TAXI
VIGNETTES

TAXI
VIGNETTES

Scenes from a San Francisco Cab
Driver 1977-1989

BILL DIETCH

PALMETTO
PUBLISHING
Charleston, SC
www.PalmettoPublishing.com

Taxi Vignettes
Scenes from a San Francisco Cab Driver, 1977-1989

Copyright © 2023 by Bill Dietch

All rights reserved.

No portion of this book may be reproduced, stored in a retrieval system, or transmitted in any form by any means—electronic, mechanical, photocopy, recording, or other—except for brief quotations in printed reviews, without prior permission of the author.

First Edition

Paperback ISBN: 979-8-8229-2524-3

Table of Contents

Introduction · vii
The Saloon · 1
Beatrice and Audrey · 4
The Leg · 7
Pants on Fire · 11
Backseat · 14
Water Broke · 18
Famous People · 21
Baby in the Projects · 24
Dinner · 27
Robbery and Revenge · 30
Santa Lucia · 33
Her Little Miracle · 36
The Amazing Mrs. Goldberg · · · · · · · · · · · · · · · · · · · 39
Evidence · 42
The Procession · 45
Marge · 48

The Gathering · 51
Too Good to Be True · 54
Hold That Thought · 57
The Party · 60
Bottoms Up · 64
Incident at City Hall · 67
Manny the Hack · 70
The News Anchors · 73
San Francisco Woman · 77
Another Day at the Office · 80

Introduction

In the 1970s and '80s, San Francisco was a very vibrant city with an abundance of creative talent. The local music scene thrived with bands like; Santana, Journey, and the Grateful Dead, to name just a few. People still wore bell bottoms, and Reeboks; they drank, "Harvey Wallbangers", and went to ball games at Candlestick Park. Streetcar rides cost a quarter, rents were mostly affordable, and the city was home to a wide variety of personalities and notable characters.

Life was much different then: It was not a "High-Tech" existence. There were no cell phones or laptops; no public "Wi-Fi" of any kind, anywhere. A remote for your TV, or an answering machine for your telephone was about as "High Tech" as it got. There were no ride-share companies, such as Uber and Lyft—Taxis still dominated that market.

Back then, driving a cab suited my personality. Not knowing who, what, where, or when, was very appealing to me; and that's exactly what a cab driver faces every shift, with every fare. In the twelve years that I drove a cab, I picked up hundreds of passengers from all walks of life—The good, the bad, and the inbetween.

These vignettes are a glimpse of people, and situations that I encountered as a taxi driver in San Francisco; and after all these years, I still treasure the experience.

The Saloon

You've got to be young and stupid, and at the time, I was both...with a vengeance. It was 1977; I was twenty-five years old and a cab driver in San Francisco. That night, I met two other cab driver friends at The Saloon, the oldest bar in the city— a serious dive bar with live blues nightly, a tiny dance floor, cheap drinks, and good music. The only drawback was the faint yet persistent smell of urine. But after a few drinks and a couple cigarettes, you hardly noticed. I was sitting at the bar with my friends when the bartender handed me a drink and said, "The woman over there bought you this." I looked over to where he pointed and saw this lovely woman smiling sheepishly at me. My friends said, "Man, you've got to go over there and thank her!"

"On my way!" I went over there and introduced myself. Her name was Gloria; we started talking and drinking and then I asked her to dance. We spent the rest of the evening dancing, drinking, and flirting like crazy. I'm thinking, *Maybe I'm gonna get lucky.*

After an hour or so, my friends decided to leave and gave me the wink that implied, "Enjoy yourself." Gloria and I stayed for another round, and she said she lived across the street in a small residential hotel on Columbus and Broadway. By now the bar was closing, and I offered to walk her home. When we arrived, she invited me up to her room. Of course, I obliged. I'm twenty-five and bulletproof with testosterone leaking from my veins. Her room overlooked Broadway with its lights and pulsing traffic below. You had a clear view of Carol Doda's neon sign with her nipples flashing on and off. It was one of the first topless joints in the country— a real cultural icon.

At this point, we're both buzzed on Jack Daniels and things were getting hot and heavy. I'm sitting on the edge of the bed in my underwear, my heart racing, taking my socks off as fast as possible, when I hear her behind me say, "Umm, Bill, there's something I think you should know." Ping! At that moment, the bells and whistles went off like fire alarms. Suddenly, I realized that the slight Adam's apple, the rather large hands, and the faint stubble above her upper lip that I seemed to dismiss in my inebriated stupor was now quite sobering. She was standing next to the dresser.

I said, "Don't worry, I get it." I started putting my socks back on as fast as possible, followed by my blue jeans. I thanked her, wished her the best, and beelined down the stairs, shoes untied, shirt untucked, till I was on the street hailing a cab. "Taxi! Taxi!"

Beatrice and Audrey

It was a gorgeous afternoon, and I could see the sun shimmering on the ocean like a painting. I had just finished lunch at a greasy spoon on Taraval Street and was sitting in my cab listening to the taxi radio. The dispatcher read off intersections like an auctioneer: "Clay and Fillmore, Turk and Taylor, 25th and Mission, California and Jones, Sutter and Montgomery," etc., etc. I heard an intersection called out in St. Francis Wood, a swanky, upscale neighborhood just blocks from where I was parked. I checked in: "Yellow Cab 551 at 19th and Taraval." The dispatcher replied, "Yellow Cab 551, get 144 St. Francis Blvd." I confirmed: "Roger, 144 St. Francis Blvd." I got to my assigned address to find a lovely two-story single-family home with a well-manicured front lawn and a black ornamental wrought iron fence surrounding the property. As I pulled up, I could see two elderly ladies, perhaps in their eighties, very well dressed with impeccable silver hair that looked like it had been coiffed that morning. I got out of the cab and opened the back door. "Good afternoon, ladies." They replied in unison, "Good afternoon!" I got them seated, introduced myself, and asked where they were going. They told me they wanted to go to a cemetery in Colma, a small town a few miles south of San Francisco that has numerous cemeteries. In fact, I don't think there is anything else in Colma other than cemeteries.

    The ladies were sisters— Beatrice and Audrey. They were very personable and a bit eccentric. They were dressed to the nines with perfectly matching wardrobes, flawless in every way. On our way to Colma, we stopped at a florist. The ladies went into the florist shop and minutes later returned with a man pushing a cartful of fresh flowers behind them. I got out of the cab and put the bouquets in the trunk. When we got back in the cab, I said, "Wow, you gals are really going all out this afternoon!" They chuckled and said, in unison, it was the least they could do.

    Once in the cemetery, they instructed me where to go, and I soon pulled over on a service road. I stopped, opened the trunk, and the sisters each pulled out the colorful bouquets and meandered to the plot they came to visit. I waited outside, leaning on the cab under the bright blue sky, and smoked a cigarette. In the distance, I could see the sisters going from one headstone to another, which seemed odd to me. I thought to myself, *These ladies seem to know a lot of people in this cemetery.* I got back in the cab, read the newspaper with the meter still running, and knew I had to take them back home. About fifteen minutes later, I saw them strolling back. When they got in the cab, Beatrice put her hand on Audrey's and said, "That was just wonderful." Audrey replied, smiling, "Why, yes, that was absolutely splendid." I commented, "I thought you were going to one gravesite, but you went to several. You two sure know a lot of people here." With a shy and somewhat mischievous giggle, they said—in unison, of course—"Oh, my dear, we don't know any of the people here, we just enjoy doing this!"

The Leg

I drove slowly in front of the Veterans building on Van Ness Avenue. I saw a man with a walker standing at attention in front of the taxi stand. He was dressed in a perfectly pressed formal Army uniform. His boots were ultra-polished with pointed toes that could kill a cockroach in a corner. He had a number of honorary medals in all colors hanging from his lapel. His uniform was a bit baggy and his beret hung slightly over one ear, but he still looked somewhat regal. He was a short and thin man, looked to be in his mid- to late-seventies. I pulled over and asked if he needed a ride. "Yep," he answered.

I got out of the cab and opened the back door for him. "How ya doin' tonight?" I asked.

"I'm going to the apartment building at Washington and Hyde." He sat down carefully on the seat with his prosthetic leg fully extended like a wooden plank. He reached into his pocket and seemed to maneuver a wire or lever of some sort. Poof! The prosthetic leg collapses, folds like a switchblade, quickly and evenly, as he swung around, putting both legs inside the cab. I put his walker in the trunk and started driving. I asked him what was going on at the Veterans building; he said it was a dinner honoring veterans who fought at the Battle of the Bulge in World War II. He continued to look straight ahead, like the disciplined soldier I imagined he had been.

We arrived at the apartment building on Hyde Street, and I drove into the circle in front of the entrance near the streetlight. I got out, retrieved his walker from the trunk, and opened the back door. I stood close to him in case he needed assistance getting out of the cab. He put his hand in his pocket again and pulled on the gadget controlling his prosthetic leg. Suddenly and unexpectedly, his leg started flailing back and forth, up and down, in and out, side to side, kicking uncontrollably like a wild stallion in heat. He stayed silent, looking straight ahead as if everything was copacetic. The poor man just sat there, stoic and muted, as he tried to gain control of his leg, a leg that seemed to have a mind of its own, a leg going awry in epic proportions.

Then without warning, a stirring sense of guilt began to overcome me, and I felt an uncontrollable urge to laugh. Yes, laugh. As a child, I had a certain propensity for laughing at inappropriate moments, and apparently that trait was still with me. *Oh please, I said to myself, Don't laugh. How dare I laugh at this man who helped save the world from evil, ensuring that I and others would live in a world free of mad men like Hitler and Mussolini. Have I no respect, no conscience, no moral character? He's a war hero, for Christ's sake!* Still, I continued silently laughing, tears running down my cheeks while my belly jiggled. People at a nearby cafe ran over to help. I hid my face in shame to avoid others from seeing what a sick and demented person I was. I felt terrible, guilty, and beyond embarrassed.

Finally, a woman from the cafe got him out of the cab and on his feet again. He stood there for a moment then reached inside his pocket. I'm thinking, *No, no, please don't make that leg go off again.* Instead, he pulls out some cash and asks me, "What do I owe you?"

I look at the cash, then look at him and say, "Please, that's OK— the ride is on me, it's the least I can do for all you've done and sacrificed."

"No, no, I insist!" He orders.

After a bumbling moment, I say, "Five bucks and we'll call it even." He pays me; I thank him and wish him a goodnight. He walks up closely to me, wearing a slight smirk, and whispers, with a wink, "Well, I won't be going dancing anytime soon."

Pants on Fire

I was working the early shift from 4:00 a.m. to 2:00 p.m. In the early morning hours, strange and bizarre rides tend to happen, and this morning was no exception. Rather than wait in line at hotels or cab stands to pick up fares, I preferred to work the taxi radio. It got me out in the neighborhoods with the locals, and I liked that better than being downtown, picking up anonymous tourists and businesspeople.

This morning, I got a radio call for 26 Fountain Street in Eureka Heights. When I pulled up to the address, I could see a light was on at the house. I sat and filled out my daily taxi log, sipping on a hot cup of coffee while I waited for my fare to come out. After a few minutes, I could see a man walking gingerly down the steps. As he got closer, I could see he looked disheveled—his pants were wet and crumpled and he was holding a towel. I thought, *Shit, it's not even sunrise and this guy looks loaded.* Picking up drunks in the cab business is nothing new; in fact, it happens quite frequently…but Jesus, it's not even daybreak yet!

    The man walks up to the cab, gets in the back seat, and commands, "Take me to the emergency room at SF General, and make it fast!" I turn around to look at him and his pants are literally soaking wet. He doesn't sound drunk, and I smell something, but it doesn't smell like booze. I start driving and ask him, "What the hell happened?" In the most pissed-off and disgusted tone, he loudly and emphatically tells me he was sitting on the toilet smoking a cigarette, reading the morning paper, when he threw the cigarette butt between his legs into the toilet bowl. Boom! The toilet exploded in flames.

    "Holy Christ," I uttered.

    With every word, he sounded angrier and more disturbed. He told me his cleaning lady was over at his house yesterday and apparently didn't flush the flammable cleaning solvent when she finished cleaning the toilet bowl. "My fucking balls are scorched, my dick is singed, and my ass is fried! Faster, driver, faster!" The poor bastard was in a lot of pain—I could smell the putrid scent of burning hair mixed with cleaning solvent.

"I can't believe this shit," he says. "I was supposed to fly to LA for a business meeting this morning. Instead, I'm headed to the emergency room with toxic solvent up my ass, and the sun's not even up! … Fucking cleaning lady."

I drive as fast as possible through the dark and empty streets till I finally get to the emergency entrance. The poor guy is moaning in agony, rocking back and forth, mumbling expletives, clutching the towel he's had in his hand. He throws a twenty over the seat and I scramble to give him his change. He gets out of the cab, wrought with pain, and hobbles to the entrance way, leaving a trail of water and cleaning solvent in his tracks. I watch him as he disappears into the brightly lit hospital. It's a little after 5:00 a.m. and I'm parked outside of the emergency entrance, sitting in silence with the windows open, recounting what just happened and waiting for the sun to rise.

Backseat

I watched her navigate the spiral stairs leading down to the sidewalk. She appeared to be in her thirties or forties and looked like an unmade bed, with her hair a mess, dirty pink sweatpants, and a stained hooded sweatshirt. I stood beside the open back door and said hello. She mumbled something incoherent then got inside the cab. I asked where she was going. "Oh, I'm not going very far; I just need you to take me to the store at Pine and Divisadero." When we got to the intersection, I asked which store she wanted to go to. She said, "That one," and pointed to the liquor store on the corner. —Somehow, that didn't surprise me. When I pulled in front of the store, she said, with a raspy voice, "Driver, could you just go in there for me and pick up a pack of Marlboro's and a fifth of Gerson's vodka?" I wasn't happy about the request, but complied, because it probably would have taken a half a day if she went in. I went inside and bought her items. A few minutes later when I returned, I opened the back door to hand her the vodka and cigarettes and was met with a stench that could gag a maggot. "What the hell?" I yelled. Sitting there next to her was the culprit. She had defecated on the seat. I looked with disbelief. "Are you fuckin' kidding me? I don't believe this!" She looked expressionless and said nothing—no apology, no explanation of any kind, not a word. I flipped out and said, "Here's your stuff, here's your change, now get the fuck outta my cab, *now*!"

"Oh please, driver," she pleaded, "could you just take me home? I'll give you a really good tip, I promise." I retorted, "Go! Get out, now." I helped her, forcefully, out of the cab. I stood there with the back door open, aghast at the steaming souvenir she left behind. After a moment of contemplation, I reached in, grabbed the underside of the seat, and yanked the entire backseat out of the cab, dragging it onto the sidewalk next to the curb. With all the windows down and the cab smelling like an outhouse, I drove away furiously, asking myself, *Is this how you really want to make a living?*

I got to the taxi yard and went to the gas pumps to fill up. Richie Gomez, the gas attendant, says to me, "You're in early today, Bill." I show him where the backseat was and give him a brief synopsis as to why I'm in early. He starts to laugh hysterically and says, "I've been working here nearly twenty years and have heard a lot of stories, but this one takes the cake." Then, out of nowhere, he says to me, "Don't look now, but here comes Steele."

    Mr. Steele was the president of Yellow Cab Company. He was a short, stocky man who wore lifts in his shoes to appear taller. He had the most insincere smile I'd ever seen and wore it constantly. He walked by and said hello to Richie as he was filling up my cab. Steele peered inside the cab inquisitively and asked where the backseat was. Richie wasn't laughing anymore and had an "uh oh" expression on his face. I told Mr. Steele that I had stopped at a corner store to get a pack of cigarettes and when I returned, the backseat was gone. He looked me dead in the eye for what seemed an eternity. "All right, let me get this straight. You stopped at a corner store to get cigarettes and when you returned, the backseat was gone. Is that what you're telling me, Mr. Dietch, is that what you're telling me?"

    "Yes, yes, exactly, someone stole the backseat." I answered. After a long and silent pause, Steele looked at me deep and hard, his squinty eyes piercing mine with contempt and disbelief. He continued, "I find this very hard to believe—it makes no sense to me."

I lied through my teeth and told him, "I'm telling you God's honest truth, sir." Steele becomes livid, his voice thickened with anger. He yells, loudly and forcefully, "Mr. Dietch, it beats the living shit out of me why anyone would want to steal a backseat out of a taxi!"
	"Me too, Mr. Steele…me too."

Water Broke

Yellow Cab Company had just gotten back in business after a year of some major restructuring. Consequently, the taxis were not in the best of shape. Many of the cabs needed wheel alignments, tires, tune-ups, hoses, belts, etc. The taxi I had on this shift felt like it had square wheels. The ride was as rough as I imagined an old stagecoach would be. The oil light came on from time to time, even though the oil had been checked that morning, and the temperature gauge light flickered intermittently as well.

  I had been a San Francisco taxi driver for a total of four shifts, and so far, nothing particularly notable had happened—this morning, that was about to change. It was about 5:00 a.m.; the dark streets were wet from the cold rain, and the fog was damp and heavy. I had just dropped off a passenger at a post office branch at 20th Avenue and Irving Street in the Sunset District. I was parked and counting my change when I got a radio call for 48th Ave. and Judah St. There was next-to-no traffic at that time and I got to the address within minutes. When I arrived, I saw a woman waddling down the driveway toward the street. She was pregnant— very, very pregnant. She squeezed into the backseat, panicky, frantic, and talking a mile a minute. "Take me to the emergency room at UC Hospital, I'm about to give birth. I called my husband, who works at UPS, and he told me to call a cab right away—he said he would meet me there. Oh my God, please go as fast as you can, driver, I'm in pain!" She was lying on her side, moaning and screaming in what must have been excruciating pain. They were sounds of agony that could only be described as deathlike—though she was about to present the opposite.

 The rain was coming down steady and the wipers struggled to keep up as they squealed and stuttered across the windshield. As I'm driving up Judah St. toward the hospital, I see that a broken-down streetcar had slowed the little traffic there was to a crawl. I told her I was going to go up one block to Kirkham St., which runs parallel to Judah and has no streetcars and fewer lights and stop signs. "No! No!" she yelled desperately. "UC Hospital is straight ahead and I'm running out of time!" I told her I was aware of that and that I was going to get her there as fast as possible. I'm going about fifty miles per hour, the cab is shaking, rocking, and rolling up Kirkham St. The front wheels feel like they're about to fall off; it's dark and the headlights hardly penetrate the fog and mist. We were about ten blocks from the hospital when she yelled, "The water broke!"

I said, "The water broke?" I'm looking at the dashboard for a red light or something that indicates the water broke. I already had issues with this cab this morning, but I don't see any lights or signs that there's a problem with the water or water pump. "How do you know the water broke?" I asked. She yelled back at me, "My water broke, *my* water broke!"

I thought, *How could I be so stupid?* I felt like a moron. Of course, *her* water broke. We got to the hospital, and I drove to the emergency entrance. She's on her back, sweating profusely, taking deep breaths and literally seconds from giving birth. I fly out of the cab and yell, "There's a woman having a baby over here and we need a doctor—fast!" Fortunately, two ambulance attendants happened to be near by and ran over to the cab, and delivered the baby. We were just in the nick of time. Immediately, the screams of pain silenced, the panicked energy subsided, my heart had begun to stop racing, and the only sounds heard were that of a newborn baby—a newborn baby girl.

Famous People

There are always famous people of one sort or another in San Francisco. I've had a number of them in my cab— writers, musicians, actors, athletes, politicians, and artists. But of all the famous people I've picked up over the years, none were more engaging than the one I was about to pick up today.

    I had just dropped off a passenger at Moffitt Hospital and got a radio call for a party named Young at the main entrance. Moments later, a couple came out, introduced themselves as the Youngs, and got in the cab. They told me they lived in La Honda, a small town about an hour south of San Francisco in the Santa Cruz Mountains, and hoped I could take them there. They were in the city visiting their son in the hospital, but their car had problems and had to be towed, so they called a taxi. I gave them a quote for the ride, and they agreed. They wanted to stop at two stores on Market Street before heading home. I parked by the stores, which were almost next to each other, and they both got out. The woman went into a store that sold high-end Japanese pottery and the man went into an electric train shop next door. About twenty minutes later, the woman returned with several bags and boxes of pottery, and the man came back with the shop owner, carrying a few large boxes of electric train items. The shop owner and I put the boxes in the trunk while the couple sat in the cab. While the trunk was open, I leaned toward the shop owner and asked, "How did this guy pay you? They want me to drive them down to La Honda and there's already twenty bucks on the meter." He replied, "Don't worry, he's Neil Young."

" Neil Young!" I yelp. "Neil Young, the musician, that Neil Young?"

"Yeah, that Neil Young," he answered.

It was a beautiful spring day, a great day for a ride down the coast with the legendary Neil Young and his wife. We drove south on Dolores Street, past the colorful Victorian houses that lined the street. The median that runs down the middle of the street was ripe with spring flowers. After a few minutes, I said, "So, I understand from the shop owner of the train store that you're Neil Young."

"Yes, that's me and always has been," he replied. I found him to be very friendly and happy to answer questions. When I asked him about the electric trains, he really lit up. He told me he was an avid model train enthusiast; in fact, he owned a stake in Lionel Trains. He mentioned that he and his sons had a large electric train set up in their house.

Their house was located in a remote part of La Honda on a dirt road that led to a large compound. It was a spacious, country-style mansion surrounded by several acres of land. When we arrived, he asked if I would like to see his electric train room. The room was huge, with what looked like miles of tracks and dozens of train cars that went through tunnels, mountains, and villages that looked literally lifelike. He donned an engineer's cap, then got behind the huge control panel to start the trains running. He was completely engaged, and I was completely enthralled like a kid in a toy store. You could tell this was a real passion for him—similar to his music and collection of guitars that were everywhere. By now, it was getting late, and I had to get the cab back to the yard. Neil tipped me generously and I thanked them both for their hospitality. We shook hands and off I went, back to the city with another notable cab story to add to my repertoire.

Baby in the Projects

Two girls flagged me down on Haight Street and wanted me to take them to the housing projects at Hayes and Buchanan. They looked like teenagers, and one of the girls was carrying a baby in what looked like a car seat for infants. When we got to their destination, I pulled into the lot, which was surrounded by a large chain-link fence, and parked in front of the building. One of the girls said, "We'll be right back, have to go up and get some money." As they both exited the cab, leaving the baby behind, I said, "Whoa, whoa, wait, one of you stay here with the baby!"

"It's OK, we'll be right back," I heard.

"No, hey, hey!" They were gone like turkeys through the corn, leaving me behind and bewildered as to what the hell I'm supposed to do with a baby in my cab—in the projects. I couldn't believe it. I'm a white cab driver, parked like a sitting duck with cash in my pocket. I'm in the middle of the projects with a Black baby in the backseat of my cab, surrounded by the riff raff of blaring boomboxes and gangsters smoking crack. What could possibly go wrong?

    Five minutes go by, then ten minutes, and now I'm seriously nervous. After fifteen excruciating minutes, I decide to try and find someone who knows this baby and the whereabouts of his mother. I put a blanket, a rattle, and a box of animal crackers that were left behind into the car seat with the baby and started walking, looking for help of any kind. I walk past a bunch of guys hanging out near one of the gated entrances and immediately hear, "Hey man, that baby don't look like you, motherfucker."

    "You a kidnapper, child molester?"

    "What da fuck you doin' here anyway, honky?"

    All eyes are on me as I make my way past them. I mentioned that I'm looking for the mother who abandoned this baby in my cab. "I think you stole that baby, motherfucker."

    Someone yells, "You a fuckin' pervert, man!" I make my way toward an area where I see some older ladies standing around. A couple of these guys are following me with menacing looks and I'm still getting pelted with profanity and threats. To say I was beginning to fear for my safety, possibly my life, would be an understatement. I walk up to the group of ladies, holding the car seat with the baby, and ask if they know who this is, and who and where the mother might be. One woman takes the car seat, and another woman says, "I know dis child, it's Caroline's grandbaby. Her daughter, Leena, ain't much older than fifteen or sixteen." I plead to anyone who will listen, "Could you please find the mother and give her back her baby?" The punks are near me now, and literally threatening to "off" me if I don't get my "white ass outta here."

Walking over now is a woman they call Auntie Cora. Everyone seems to know her, and she appears to wield authority and respect, including from the punks breathing down my neck. She's a middle-aged woman of rather large stature, and when she speaks, everyone listens. You don't mess with Auntie Cora. "Give me dat child, I'll bring him to Leena and give her a piece of my mind too! And you ruffians can crawl back in yo holes and let this man alone! Do I make myself clear?" The young dudes completely change their tone and do what she says with obedience and acquiescence. I thank Auntie Cora profusely and tell her I don't know what would have happened if she hadn't come around. She scolds me, "Don't waste yo' time thankin' me, boy, just get yo' sorry ass on outta here an' best not come back, ya hear? Go!"...I go.

DINNER

Her name was Camille. I had picked her up in the Financial District a couple times in the past and found her very attractive and quite charming. I recall wanting to ask her out, but thought, *Why would a beautiful woman like her, who no doubt makes more money in a day than I make in a week, be interested in me, a cab driver? She probably goes out with a guy who drives a Porsche, makes six figures, and wears a Rolex and wingtips.* I saw her trying to hail a cab from across Battery St. and quickly honked the horn and flicked the headlights to get her attention. She saw me and waved her hand in acknowledgement. I jostled the cab through the bustling traffic like a slalom skier headed toward the finish line. I pulled up, and she got in and said, "Hi!" with a big smile that showed off her near-perfect teeth and sensuous lips. "Hi!" I said. "Good to see you again, where ya headed?"

"Good to see you too! I have to go to the Medical Arts building on Sutter St." We continued to chat and chortle till we got to her destination. While she fiddled through her purse for cash to pay me, I decided to ask her out, figuring I had nothing to lose. I asked her if she wanted to go for dinner Friday night. "I'd love to!" she answered. "Do you have a place in mind?"

I thought, *Jesus, did I just hear her right? That was harmless!* "How 'bout Castellano's on Union St. in North Beach?" North Beach is the Italian section of the city.

"I've heard of that restaurant," she said, "but never eaten there; that would be wonderful."

"Great; I'll make reservations for eight o'clock and meet you there."

"Perfect! I'll be looking forward to seeing you then, Bill." She got out of the cab and sashayed up the steps to the entrance of the building. I was thrilled, excited, and couldn't wait till Friday evening.

It was just before eight when I got to Castellano's. I saw Camille walking up Union St. toward the restaurant. She was wearing a beige cashmere sweater with a black collar and black slacks that looked like she had been poured into them. The closer she got, the more beautiful she appeared. She met me at the front door, where we embraced and went inside. Her scent was alluring. The host escorted us to a small table in the corner with a checkered linen tablecloth, perfectly folded white linen napkins, and a pair of dimly lit candles. Very romantic. Camille looked beautiful, gorgeous, drop-dead gorgeous. She had long, henna-colored hair and deep-set green eyes that were almost mesmerizing. We babbled over a glass of pinot noir and Italian bread sticks with warm olive oil. I was smitten already, and from her body language, she appeared to be as well.

Then, unbelievably, when her linguini arrived, she started to devour it like a buzzsaw or a piranha. I was in shock, seriously! I couldn't believe my eyes, I had never seen anything like this before. There were clumps of parmesan lodged in her teeth, traces of marinara sauce splattered on her sleeve, and specks of fresh oregano stuck to the corners of her lips. Those teeth! That smile! The lips! What the hell just happened? She went from flirtatious eye contact to an intense, dare I say neurotic, fixation on the Italian porcelain where the linguini was. I didn't know how to react. All I knew was that my smitten feeling quickly dissipated with every forkful of food she ingested. I had begun to feel a deep sense of disappointment and wished I were anywhere but here. What I really wanted to say to her was, "Uh, sorry Camille, I have to go now; I've got to rearrange the deckchairs on the Titanic"—but I didn't.

Robbery and Revenge

It was mid-December and the streets were adorned with holiday decor. My shift was nearly over, and I figured this would be my last fare. He was a young man—looked to be in his early twenties. I picked him up at the corner of 5th and Bryant St. He wanted to go to the Tenderloin, a downtrodden neighborhood with plenty of drug dealers, hookers, homeless, and an array of street people looking desperate and lost. We made three stops, all within a block or two of each other, and I could only imagine what transpired. He returned from his final stop and said he wanted me to drop him off at a housing project in an alley south of Market Street. It was a large brick building with a huge black steel fence around it—reminiscent of a prison. I pulled up, parked in front of the building, and turned the meter off. He fumbled around for some money as I recorded the ride's info in my taxi log. While I was writing, he reached over the seat, pulled my head back violently, put the dull side of a knife blade to my throat and told me to give him all my money— not being in a negotiable position, I did exactly that. He took the money and bolted from the cab, ran down the alley, and disappeared into the night. I sat there, stunned, shocked, and nearly sick to my stomach. My heart pounded like a jackhammer, and I felt an overwhelming sense of despair and defeat. In almost ten years of driving a cab, I had never been robbed. The feeling was beyond words. I felt like I was robbed of more than my money. The very essence of me felt violated to the core.

    On an early spring day in April, I was driving down 4th St. near Folsom, when out of the corner of my eye, I saw the son of a bitch standing at a bus stop across the street. My heart began to pound as my eyes became fixed on him like a hawk on its prey. I drove up on the curb and parked slightly on the sidewalk, then I popped the hood and turned the flashers on, as if I had mechanical problems. I grabbed the large black steel flashlight from my seat, the kind cops carry, and hustled my way across the bustling street as fast as I could. He was standing at the bus stop, unaware that I had him in my sights. I'm in full stride when he finally sees me and takes off running through the gas station toward the same alley where he robbed me. I'm running full tilt behind him when my beloved tweed cap flies off; I keep running. Except for him, everything appears to be bright white and in slow motion. I see nothing, I hear nothing—no traffic, no horns, no people, just the sound of my shoes slapping the pavement. We're running down the alley and I'm just feet behind him when he vaults to the steel fence, trying to escape my pursuit. He starts to climb, and I lunge and grab his pant leg, pulling him down to the ground. My heart feels like it's gonna explode. He attempts to get up and run when I whack him in the knee with the steel flashlight. He screams in pain and falls down, gasping for air. I grab him by his hair and punch him a couple times in the nose. I get him on his feet and warn him, "I'll break your fuckin' kneecaps if you make any attempts to run." I'm half Sicilian, after all.

    Two boys playing in the alley start to give me a hard time and ask what I'm doing. I flash my taxi badge and tell them, "I'm a cop and this man is under arrest. Now go play in the traffic and let me do my job." I'm shaking like a leaf, trying to catch my breath as I walk him toward my cab. We walk through the gas station where I see my tweed cap and retrieve it. I march him like a prisoner across 4th St. to my cab and throw him in the trunk. I drove to the main police station, pulled him out of the trunk and took him inside. Then I filed an incident report and asked myself, "Is revenge sweet?" Today, it was like honey.

Santa Lucia

Bixby was a short, wiry man with salt and pepper hair and horn-rimmed sunglasses that sat cock-eyed on his nose. His wife, Pauline, was sweet and shy with a short pixie and a lovely smile. They were from Chicago, where they met at the art institute. She had been a sculptor, and he an opera singer. They were middle-aged and inseparable, always engaging in loving banter—a real love story for the ages. I had picked them up several times over the years. Both were frail, nearly blind, and in questionable health. They frequently called for a cab to take them to one clinic or another for various health issues. Bixby could be salty at times. He always had salacious stories of his days before Pauline. She would sit patiently, quietly smiling while he would spin tales of days gone by. They never stopped holding hands and he constantly complimented her with sweet phrases of affection. I dropped them off at a clinic on Geary Blvd. and helped them out of the cab. I took Bixby's arm, he took Pauline's, and together we walked slowly and cautiously to the entrance with their matching striped walking sticks in hand—it was always a pleasure to see them. They were good people.

It had been a couple years since I had them in my cab and occasionally they would cross my mind. Today, I happened to get a radio call for their address. I arrived at their apartment building and waited for them to come out. A few minutes later, Bixby came out alone. I hurried up the entrance way to meet him. "Good morning, Bixby!"

"Good morning," he echoed.

"Do you know who I am?" I asked. He hesitated for a moment, then answered, "I think I do; you're Bill, right?" It always amazed me how he could identify someone in just a few syllables.

I helped him into the cab and asked, "Where's the better half this morning?" After a brief pause, he said, "Well, Bill, Pauline passed away last year."

"I'm so sorry to hear this, Bixby." And I was; she was a very warm and gentle soul.

"Thank you, he said. "It's been difficult."

"I'm sure it has been," I acknowledged.

TAXI VIGNETTES

I drove down Harrison Street, past a playground and the ballpark next to it, when I heard the sounds of someone singing. Bixby heard the singing too, and told me, "One of the hardest things is not being able to sing to Pauline. She loved to be serenaded." I asked what songs he sang to her. "Actually, just one, Bill, her favorite." Another brief pause ensued. Then, to my astonishment and surprise, he broke out in song. It was "Santa Lucia." My ears perked up as I listened intently. After a moment, my heart began to flutter, my throat tightened, and I choked up. I had never heard anything so beautiful in my life. His voice was clear and distinctive. His vibrato gave me chills as he sang with pure passion and clarity. He sang with a resonance I imagined Pauline could hear. I was moved to tears. When he finished singing, he declared with devotion, "I loved that woman with every note I sang to her."

Her Little Miracle

The house was a Queen-Anne-style mansion that sat firmly on the side of a hill in Ashbury Heights. When I pulled up in front, I saw a young boy about ten years old standing on the porch. He was dressed in a beige double-breasted coat with neatly pressed khaki pants and brown shoes, buffed and polished. He was wearing a tan wool cap with a short visor in the front and looked like he was going to a formal event, perhaps a wedding or debutante ball. When he saw me, he walked down the steps with perfect posture and a stride of confidence beyond his age. "Good afternoon," he greeted. "My name is Duncan Calloway, and I'm waiting for my mother to come out. We're going to the airport to meet my dad, who's flying in from the Philippines—he's a diplomat for the government."

"Good afternoon, Duncan, pleasure to meet you."

TAXI VIGNETTES

He saw his mother come out the front door and quickly scurried up the steps, took her arm, and escorted her down to the taxi. He opened the back door, held her hand, and helped her in. "Are you in all right, mother?"

"Yes, Duncan, thank you, dear," she answered. He closed her door and got in the other side. I thought, *What a perfect little gentleman.* He called her mother—very formal.

I introduced myself and told the mother, "You've got quite the little man there." She smiled and rolled her eyes, "Yes, indeed I do. I'm not sure where he gets his formal and proper behavior, but he's been like this almost from the cradle. My husband jokes that they must have switched the cribs in the nursery, because no one in our family on either side behaves this way!"

"Well, I guess you hit the jackpot," I said. As I headed to the airport, I continued talking with the mother while Duncan was absorbed with a Rubik's Cube. She told me Duncan was eleven years old, very friendly, and very good in school. She said he was sensitive and helpful, both at home and at school. "He loves dinosaurs and playing tag with the kids in the lot down the street."

I said, "It sounds like you're very lucky to have such a special son."

"Yes, I suppose I am," she replied.

I was stopped in heavy traffic on the corner of Duboce Avenue and Division Street, headed for the freeway. Across the street at the corner was an elderly lady in a wheelchair, trying to get up over the curb and out of the traffic. She had a beat-up wool blanket around her with a wooden cane resting across her legs. She tried repeatedly to lift and push her way over the curb. Cars were driving by and pedestrians were crossing the street, but nobody seemed to notice, or at least bothered to help her.

"Mother, look, that woman is struggling to get her wheelchair over the curb, and nobody is helping her."

"Yes, I see that, Duncan."

"Someone should help her!" he shouted. "She needs help!" Then suddenly, in a flash, Duncan opened the door and rushed across the street through the stalled traffic. He pushed the woman and her wheelchair up over the curb to safety. I watched him bend down and ask her if she was all right, putting his hand reassuringly on her shoulder. She smiled and folded her hands in grace to thank him, then Duncan started walking back through the line of cars to the cab. The mother choked up. She pulled a tissue from her purse, wiped the tears from her eyes and murmured, "He's my little miracle, my little miracle."

The Amazing Mrs. Goldberg

I had dropped off a passenger at the airport and was headed back to the city when I got a radio call for an address in Park Merced, a residential neighborhood near the county line. An elderly woman, maybe in her late seventies, came out of the high-rise, walking toward my cab. I opened the back door and waited for her to get in. She had a bright smile and was wearing a dark red floral coat with a matching scarf. She was holding a red purse in one hand and a cane in the other. She got inside, and asked, "How are you doing this lovely afternoon?" Immediately, I could tell she had a friendly and vivacious personality. She wanted to go to Macy's on Union Square to pick up some gifts for the holidays. She asked if I would wait for her and bring her back home, making this a very lucrative ride—I told her I would.

    Her name was Mrs. Goldberg and she started telling me her life story. She was born in Poland and came to New York City as a young woman. She worked in the garment district, where she met her husband who happened to be a musician with the Cab Calloway Orchestra. They had two sons and moved to San Francisco in the mid-1950s. After her sons grew up, she and her husband traveled the world. They visited world-class museums, took boat rides down the Seine, attended ballets and concerts, and rubbed shoulders with the likes of Duke Ellington and Louis Armstrong. She told me her husband passed away many years ago and left her money he had inherited from his family. She joked, "It has been a good life, Bill, but I spend a small fortune on taxis!" She seemed so positive, so happy and pleasant. I was struck by her upbeat nature.

    I dropped her off at Macy's, parked in the passenger zone, and told her I'd be here waiting. After a short while, she returned with some packages and got back in the cab. She looked at her watch and asked me if I had time to join her for a drink at The Cliff House, a restaurant at the beach with a stunning view of the Pacific Ocean. Apparently, that was a daily ritual for her around this time. I laughed and said, "Sure, why not?" She was so charming and delightful, how could I say no?

When we got to The Cliff House, I helped her out of the cab and we walked inside to a table by the window overlooking the ocean. She ordered a gin and tonic with a twist and offered to buy me a drink. I ordered a cappuccino. She continued to tell me how wonderful life had been for her, how grateful she was for all the amazing experiences she'd had and how proud she was of her sons. I loved listening to her; she was an inspiration. We gazed out over the shimmering water, watching the seagulls dance like ballerinas in the afternoon sun, and then it was time to go.

We walked back to the cab, and I drove her home. I thanked her for her joyful company, wonderful stories, and vibrant outlook on life. It had been such a pleasure to meet her. I got out of the cab and opened her door. When I reached for her hand, her coat sleeve had rolled up enough for me to catch a glimpse of a faded tattoo with numbers on her forearm. The Holocaust, I figured. I was shocked and saddened. I could feel my eyes bulging out as I gawked at her arm. Mrs. Goldberg looked passively at me and said, "Oh, that. It's from another time—a time I will never forget, a time I will forever remember, but a time I refuse to dwell on."

EVIDENCE

He was tall and handsome, with broad shoulders and a well-manicured beard. He was very well dressed and looked to be in his forties. I got the impression he was a professional with money and perhaps status of some sort. But there was something about this guy that seemed troubling.

I picked him up on Polk St. near Broadway in front of Tamarack's Bar. It was around nine at night and the weekend was just getting started. When he got in the cab, he seemed angry, depressed, and maybe a little drunk. I tried to make small talk with him but he wasn't interested. He wanted to go to Shirley's on Fillmore St., a bar with a small patio and outdoor seating in front. As we drove toward the Marina District, he told me, "She lies to me and I can't take it anymore. I've given her every benefit of the doubt, but now I'm done with that. I know she's cheating on me, and I know who the motherfucker is. She's my wife and I've given her everything she's wanted: cars, jewelry, vacations to Mexico and Hawaii, everything money can buy. But she's an ungrateful bitch, a liar, and a cheat, and now I've finally had enough with her." I'm thinking, *I'm a cab driver, not a marriage counselor.* I wasn't about to try and console him.

I got to Fillmore Street in the Marina District and parked across the street from Shirley's. He pulled out a small piece of paper and said, "See this? I found this note in her purse yesterday." He shows me the note with the address of Shirley's written on it, the "other" guy's name, and the time she was meeting him. "Evidence." he announces. "Pure and simple. Evidence. She's a fucking whore and it's taken me years to admit that, but that's exactly what she is—a whore." I sat there waiting for him to pay me and get out, but he had other plans. He tells me, "Just wait here a minute." He leaves me a ten-dollar bill and exits the cab, struts across the street through the patio, and heads inside the bar. I was tempted to drive off, but I didn't. Why people share their darkest thoughts, their illicit secrets, and their dirty laundry with an anonymous cab driver, I'll never know—but they do.

About ten minutes later, I see him standing across the street, locked arm-in-arm with a young woman I assume is his wife. She's a tall blonde with long legs wearing a short denim skirt, a white halter top, and sandals. She's definitely a looker, brimming with sensuous beauty and oozing unbridled sexuality. She seems to have a certain aura, suggesting one man would never be enough to satisfy her carnal needs and desires. I could only imagine how he let her lustful and lascivious looks obsess him, dominate his thoughts, and stoke his paranoia.

They get in the cab and they're actually affectionate with each other. I'm somewhat surprised, given all the venom he's spewed and unleashed about her. I listen to his surrendered voice mouthing passively to her. He sounds like a prisoner of love to a sultry and seductive woman who's got him by the short and curlies. Evidence or no evidence, she has him under her thumb, and he doesn't have the gumption, strength, or fortitude to leave her. He seems a hostage to his manliness, held in a prison of his own making. As I drove to their apartment in Pacific Heights, I could see in the rearview mirror that they're making out like bandits. She was all over him like a cheap suit. She spoke softly and said, "You didn't have to break a bottle over his head, Tony, you could've killed him."

The Procession

This afternoon, there was a ton of traffic, and my passenger was ten minutes late to Oakland. Mr. Patterson was a venture capitalist on his way to a business meeting he claimed he couldn't miss. He could talk the ass off of a brass monkey and seemed to have an obnoxious arrogance about him, like a spoiled and pompous preppie. As we headed out of downtown on our way to the Bay Bridge, he bored me with his endless list of financial accomplishments and not once spoke a word other than about himself. He talked incessantly. Traffic is bad in general, but Fridays are a bitch, and this guy is in a big hurry to get to his important meeting. "Driver, can't you go any faster? I'm already late."

I held my tongue and said, "I'll do my best." On the Bay Bridge, traffic moved, but it was slow. One lane was closed, and I could tell he was getting more impatient. We finally got off the bridge and onto the freeway, headed toward downtown Oakland. About a half a mile later, traffic slowed to a crawl and Mr. Patterson began to get agitated. "Jesus Christ! What the hell is going on?" There were no accidents or road construction that I could see. "I don't know," I answered. "Looks like there might be a funeral procession up ahead." There was.

    The procession was for Felix Winchell, a ruthless drug dealer from Oakland who controlled the cocaine and crack market with an iron fist. His name appeared frequently in the news for ordering the killings of anyone who dared infringe on his monopoly. He spent years in and out of prison and was celebrated with fanfare from those who kowtowed to him. He drove flashy Lincolns with bright chrome wheels and whitewalls. He dressed in wide brim hats with full length coats, surrounded by bodyguards and fast women. But like every gregarious gangster, he eventually got whacked.

    The police closed off an entire lane on Highway 17 to accommodate the enormous procession for Mr. Winchell. There was a mile-long parade of fancy cars with their headlights on, headed to the funeral parlor. As we trudged slowly in the lane next to the steadily moving procession, Mr. Patterson, who was nearly beside himself by now, suggested I turn my headlights on and slip into the lane with the procession. "Are you serious?" I asked.

"Yes, just veer into the lane and follow the procession till we get to the 14th Street exit and then get out." At the time, we didn't know this was the procession for Felix Winchell's funeral. I thought about his suggestion for a moment, weighing the pros and cons, and decided to do it. I was as anxious to get him out of my cab as he was to get to his meeting. I waited for the motorcycle cop next to us to move on and then swung to the rear of the procession and got in with my headlights on. We drove unnoticed behind the large fleet of mourners till we reached 14th Street in downtown Oakland. I got out of the procession and headed for the office building Mr. Patterson wanted to go to. He proclaimed, "Now that wasn't so difficult, was it? If we hadn't done that, we'd still be sitting in traffic on the highway." I finally reached Mr. Patterson's destination. I pulled in front of the entrance and turned off the meter at $18.00 even. He handed me a twenty, then, unashamed, he waited for his change.

MARGE

I knew her only by her voice. She was the radio dispatcher on the morning shift at Yellow Cab. I learned she had been doing this since the early 1960s, and she was the consummate pro. Over the years, I had developed a good working relationship with Marge—that helps when you're depending on radio calls for your income. Her voice was deep and raspy, probably from smoking cigarettes for years. She had an on-air demeanor of grace under fire, steady as a rock. The morning rush hours were extremely busy, with dozens of calls an hour for taxis throughout the city. Many calls were for regular riders who depended on cabs to get them to work or other scheduled appointments. She took her job seriously and didn't take shit from anybody. She could call off intersections fast and furious, yet always articulate and precise. When she assigned you a fare, you could be sure she got the street, the address, and any special directions absolutely correct on the first go-around. Marge was all business with no jive and little patience with those who didn't do right by her. If she found you were trustworthy and reliable, she would take care of you and assign fares that were lucrative, i.e., to the airport or other long rides. If she found that you would lie about your location or didn't show up for a pickup, she would be deaf to your voice and unapologetic for it. Marge was the dispatcher's dispatcher. She was all business—nothing more, nothing less.

    In her mind, there were only two kinds of cab drivers: the ones who waited in lines at hotels, cab stands, the airport, etc. and let chance or the roll of the dice determine their income. And the hustlers who were out in the neighborhoods, listening diligently to radio calls and answering them reliably, keeping their meters ticking, generating money all through their shift. Those were "her" people, "her" soldiers. You take care of me, I take care of you. She took no kickbacks, no greasing her palms, no sir; just hard work and hustle.

    I had worked the radio religiously and got to know almost every nook and cranny of San Francisco. Over the years, I spent hours on the radio, exchanging addresses and such with Marge. We became dependent on each other, answering calls that benefited the both of us. She never knew my name or who I was. She knew me only as Yellow Cab #551, and like a nickname, she would address me as "51" on the air. When you pressed the button on the microphone, your cab number lit up on a screen in the dispatch office. After many years of working reliably together, most of the time when I checked in for an order, that's all I had to do: press the button. I didn't have to utter a word. She knew I was where I checked in and needed no more than to see my number light up on her screen—we were in sync.

One afternoon, I was in line at the gas pumps, talking with some fellow cab drivers, when a plain, nondescript middle-aged woman with gray hair in a bun walked by. One of the guys pointed and said, "That's Marge, the dispatcher." I had never seen her before. She was through with her shift and walking to her car. I decided to go over and introduce myself to her.

"Marge?" She paused, then slowly turned around and looked at me. I said, "Hi Marge, my name is Bill. You know me as 551, thought I'd introduce myself." She stood motionless with a cigarette dangling from her lips and seemed about as interested in me as contracting malaria. She looked at me blankly, then blew a breath full of smoke my way and said, "Oh." I stood there in silence for an awkward moment and then figured she was just all business, nothing more, nothing less...that was Marge.

The Gathering

Every now and then, I'd get together with a few cab drivers after work at Hank's Hospitality House, a local bar not far from the taxi yard. We'd meet and swap cab stories. Some of these guys were characters in their own right, like Bob, a.k.a. Two Notes, a tall lanky guy with a long red beard and a generous personality. He was originally from Texas and had a keen ear for music. In the early mornings, he would park his cab in front of the phone booth at 24th and Church Street. He'd tune into the morning show on KFOG, a radio station that played classic rock and roll. At that hour, the regular DJ would play two notes from a song and say, "The first caller who identifies this song gets a pair of front row tickets for a concert at the Bill Graham Auditorium." Bob would invariably listen intently, identify the notes, then frantically sprint to the phone booth, drop a dime, and name the tune. He was truly a master at this, scoring tickets repeatedly, then giving them away, to the surprise of his passengers.

Phil Dixon was in his mid-fifties and had been a cabbie for over twenty-five years. He was the oldest and most seasoned hack I knew. He had been around, and swore he had seen everything twice. The other day, a woman who was taking her poodle to the vet proved him wrong. He told us that the dog was barking incessantly, jumping all around in the backseat, and was completely out of control. But mysteriously, every few minutes the dog would collapse in silence. Phil asked the woman what was up with her dog. She answered apologetically, "My dog suffers from narcolepsy." She said she even gave him coffee in the morning, "but nothing helped!" Phil confessed, "I swear, in all my years driving a cab, that was one thing I'd never seen or heard before."

Then there was Ray, a short, husky guy with a limp who had a way of telling stories with animation and humor. He had a gambling jones and would often drive his cab straight to the racetrack, down in San Mateo and spend hours betting on the horses. In the summer, he would take a couple weeks off to hit the horseshoe circuit and compete with some of the best horseshoe players in the country. Today, he told us about a nun he had in his cab who suffered a gastrointestinal emergency and needed to "go" immediately.

Fortunately, they were driving through Golden Gate Park, where Ray was able to stop and let her out near the windmills. He said, "Here I am with a nun dressed in a full habit who probably wouldn't say shit if she had a mouthful, when suddenly she's in gastric distress!" He told us, "She grabbed her purse and ran to the grass near the windmill, copped a squat with her long black robe surrounding the event, and did her thing." Ray mentioned that the grass was damp, and she became engulfed in such a cloud of steaming condensation that you could hardly see her veil. When the nun got back in the cab, she was breathing heavily, and sighed, "Good Lord! Can you imagine if this happened on the Golden Gate Bridge?"

Too Good to Be True

Glenn lived in Bernal Heights and occasionally I would take him to the airport. He had my phone number and would call me instead of the cab company to make an appointment for the ride—this would happen a few times a year. On our way to the airport, I asked Glenn where he was flying to. He said, "Reno."

I asked what he was going there for. "To play the slots." He told me he had been a slot machine mechanic at Harrah's Casino for several years before moving to San Francisco. He said he knew all the machines and which ones had the best mechanical cylinders for winning. I said, "Are you kidding me?"

He replied, "No, I've worked on all of them and know their inner workings like the back of my hand. I've pulled every one of them apart and put them back together, knowing which were the ones to play. I've made a small fortune there."

TAXI VIGNETTES

"That's incredible," I said. "I've never heard of such a thing." He showed me a list of serial numbers that could be found on the sides of the machines, and those were the "winners." Then he mentioned, "If you like, I'll write them down for you and you can go to Reno sometime and check them out. But you should go there soon before the machines are replaced."

I admitted, "I'm not much of a gambler, but sure, why not?"

A few months later, I decided to fly to Reno with Glenn's list. I took a cab from the Reno airport to Harrah's Casino. I stopped at the bar for a drink before heading to the slot machines. I chatted with the bartender, who told me to make sure I kept enough cash in my shoe for the flight back to San Francisco. He said, "Believe me, I've seen many gamblers lose their shirts and get stuck here, broke, without a penny."

"OK," I said, and heeded his advice.

I walked inside the casino and found one of the machines from Glenn's list. I sat down and dropped a few silver dollars and lost. I went to another machine from the list and lost again. I was starting to feel a little disappointed but went to another machine, also from the list. I dropped a five-dollar coin, pulled the lever, and boom, the machine dumped a slew of coins into the chrome dish. I did it again, and again the coins came tumbling out like magic. This continued for quite a while, and eventually, cocktail waitresses started buzzing around me like bees in a hive, asking if they could get me a drink. Over the next few hours, coins were pouring out of this machine like a spigot. Prostitutes were propositioning me left, right, and center as if I were a fat cat brimming with cash. I couldn't believe it! Glenn wasn't kidding; he knew his stuff. This went on for hours. I had won hundreds of dollars and tipped as if I were a millionaire.

    Then reality started to rear its ugly head. I began to lose, but still continued feeding the slots to keep my winnings from slipping away. Over and over, I dropped coins in the slot but kept losing. No matter what I gambled, my fortune continued to dwindle. By now, the cocktail waitresses had disappeared and found another winner to court. The prostitutes abandoned me like I had the plague. I checked my funds and was nearly broke. I thought, *The machines were working right, but I didn't have that gambler's savvy or intuition.* I remembered the bartender who told me about keeping enough money in your shoe for the flight back and was glad I listened to him. It was getting late, and I didn't have enough cash to catch a cab to the airport, so I had to take a bus. I was thinking that in the midst of my gambling delusions, I should've reminded myself, "If it seems too good to be true, it's probably too good to be true," — but somehow, it doesn't work that way.

Hold That Thought

Ginny could talk a blue streak sometimes and it could be difficult to get a word in edgewise. But when you spoke, she would listen to you with an intensity beyond description. She would hang on every word, every syllable, every dangling participle that spilled from your lips, no matter what the subject. She had this unique ability to tune into what you were saying in a way that seemed unearthly. She would pay attention to you one hundred percent, as if nothing and nobody else existed. I never met anyone quite like her.

She lived in the Haight-Ashbury neighborhood and was a nurse at Ft. Miley Hospital, a veterans' facility at 43rd and Clement Street. She had a standing order with the cab company three days a week at 9:30 a.m. Occasionally, I would pick her up and take her to work. Ginny was very pretty and had a captivating smile and a very engaging personality. She was probably ten years older than me. Although she could talk, it was never incessant or obnoxious and I grew to like her—a lot. She always asked how I was and what I thought about this or that. She seemed genuinely interested and made you feel like she cared what you were thinking and feeling. After a few rides, I found myself very attracted to her. There was something about Ginny I couldn't explain, something paradoxical. I always felt she knew I had a crush on her by the way she would smile at me, tilting her head slightly, wisping her long brown hair to the side with her fingers and winking discreetly—she could be very flirtatious.

    One morning, I had been thinking of Ginny and decided to park in front of her apartment building around 9:30 a.m. to pick her up. When the dispatcher called her address, I checked in and got the order. Moments later, she hopped in the cab, said hello, and commented about what a lovely morning it was. She briefed me about her upcoming shift and what she had to do. Then she asked, "So, how are you this morning? It's always a pleasure having you as my driver. What have you been doing since I last saw you?" I told her about a trip to Europe that I was planning for the summer. She leaned up close to the front seat as if to hear me better.

As I spoke, I could sense her big brown eyes fixed on me, listening intently to each and every word I said, as if I were the only person on earth. Her arm was stretched out over the seat close to my shoulder and I could smell the sweet scent of her perfume, which only fueled my infatuation. We drove through Golden Gate Park, past the tennis courts, the museum, and the rose garden, till we got to the entrance of the medical center. I got out of the cab, opened her door, and took a deep breath to try to compose myself. I was finally going to tell Ginny my feelings, confess my strange attraction to her, and reveal my heart's true colors. She stepped out of the cab, paid me, and just when I was about to speak, she gently put her finger to my lips, as if she knew exactly what I was about to say, and whispered, "Hold that thought," then walked away…leaving me speechless.

The Party

My good friend Dan called and asked if I could fill his shift for him one Saturday night. I normally don't work Saturdays but told him I would. It was the 4 p.m. to 2 a.m. shift—a lucrative time for a Saturday night. I went down to the taxi yard, checked in around four, and was out and about shortly after. It was the middle of winter and darkness descended on the city early, leaving the streets looking both bright and dark. Unlike the day shift, there were no rides to courthouses, banks, businesses, and medical clinics. Instead, I had rides to and from theaters, nightclubs, restaurants, etc. Business was brisk. Around ten thirty, I decided to stop for a slice at Arinell's Pizza on Valencia Street. When I went back to my cab, I saw three girls up the street, trying to hail a taxi. I drove up, pulled over, and let them in. They were very friendly and seemed about my age. They said they were going to a party on Linda St., not far away in the Mission District. When I got there, they invited me to join them. They told me their friend was having a party for her sister who was visiting from Boston. I had been driving for over six hours and thought, *OK, I'll stop in for a bit and check it out.*

    The house was a three-story Victorian and the party was on the top floor. As we walked up the long, creaky flight of stairs, you could hear people talking, laughing, and carrying on. There was the music of Santana playing in the background. I could smell the scent of Mexican food and marijuana as we got closer to the apartment. When we got inside, there were party decorations everywhere and the rooms were lit with dim red lighting, and yellow crepe paper hung from the ceilings. There was a long rectangular table with an array of food and booze, with people hovering around it. Everybody seemed festive and in the partying spirit. My passengers introduced me to several people, and I was welcomed with open arms—literally. I went over to the table with the refreshments and grabbed what I thought was a glass of sangria from the punchbowl.

    A young woman named Diane came up to me and introduced herself. She was the visiting sister from Boston. She was petite, wearing a light blue sequined blouse and white jeans. We sat on a cushioned window seat in the front room and chatted about Boston and San Francisco. She was very friendly and asked me questions about living in the city and being a cab driver. About ten minutes later, I began to feel a little strange—not bad or sick, just not normal. Diane smiled affectionately and asked, "Are you OK?"

    I said, "For one glass of sangria, I'm feeling uncharacteristically buzzed."

    She said, "That's probably from the sangria, it's spiked with acid. There's a sign taped on the punchbowl that says 'S.W.A.'—spiked with acid."

    "Oh, that's great," I said, "I never noticed it. How the hell am I supposed to drive?"

    By now, it was well after midnight. I had lost all sense of time and everything in the room resembled a Salvador Dalí painting. I had begun to hallucinate. Someone dropped a cigarette from their lips and it appeared to fall in slow motion, sparks exploding wildly off the hardwood floor. The walls started bulging like pigs in a python. Voices sounded slow and slurred. Somehow, I still had a foot in reality and staggered down the stairs to the cab. The cab yard wasn't far away, and by hook or by crook I was determined to make it back. After I returned the cab, I ambled to my car in the parking lot and slept there till morning, or at least tried to.—The next day, Dan called to see how my shift went. With the sangria still churning in my system, my senses far from normal, and my perceptions still askew, I was completely baffled by his question, and asked, "Shift? What shift?"

Bottoms Up

Lars Johannson owned the Bottoms Up club at 16th and Connecticut St. It was a bar and grill just walking distance from the cab company. Sometimes I would go there after work and meet up with some other cabbies for a drink. I got to know Lars pretty well over the years; he was a good guy. Everybody liked him and he was quick with a joke. I always cashed my check there on Fridays and would have lunch a couple times a week there too. Lars was a big man with a square jaw and large hands. He had been a furniture maker back in Denmark, where he was from. He'd been living in San Francisco since the 1950s and owned his club for many years. He had a softball team called the Bottom Ups that played in citywide tournaments every year. Dust-covered trophies lined the back bar from championships the team won over the years. One of the attractions in the bar was an antique jukebox that played great tunes from the '50s and '60s. There were two TVs perched over the bar that frequently had a ball game on, and there was an old billiards table in the back. The place was usually filled with a diverse mix of people from the neighborhood.

    One night, I was driving past a hotel at 10th and Market when I saw a tall woman in a lavender wool coat, walking briskly with what looked like a broken high-heeled shoe. She waved for me to pick her up. I pulled over and she hobbled to the cab and got in. I asked where she was going, and she told me 16th and Connecticut. I asked how she was doing but she didn't reply. I could see she was looking down a lot and sensed she was somehow uncomfortable. She was tall, with broad shoulders, a square jaw, and large hands. When she spoke, her voice was deep and masculine. I looked at her in the rearview mirror several times and thought she looked somehow familiar. Then I noticed she seemed to have similar features to Lars, from the Bottoms Up club. I realized she wanted to go to the same intersection where Lars's club was and that she had an uncanny resemblance to him. I thought, *This can't be a mere coincidence. I'm almost positive this is Lars.* I kept driving and thinking, *Do I say anything? I don't want to embarrass him but how could he not know that I know it's him?* It was a very awkward and weird situation. I knew Lars lived above the bar, and when I got to 16th Street, he asked me to drop him off at the side entrance. I pulled over and parked while he went through a black leather handbag for money. He pulled out a ten-dollar bill, handed it to me, and hurriedly hopped out of the cab, limping to the side door holding the broken shoe, and went inside.

    About a week later, I went into the bar to cash my check as I always did. I didn't have any idea how Lars was going to react. I decided I would just play dumb and act like nothing happened. When I walked in, it was about 4 p.m. and the place was relatively quiet. I sidled up to the bar, said hello to Lars, and ordered a beer. I asked him to cash my check as I normally do on Fridays. Lars came back a few minutes later, leaned over the bar, handed me my money, and softly said, "Bill, I would appreciate it greatly if you didn't mention the other night to anybody, it's really quite embarrassing." I said, "Lars, I promise I'll keep it under my hat and not say a word." He smiled slyly at me and quipped, "Kinda gives a whole new meaning to 'Bottoms Up,' doesn't it?"

Incident at City Hall

It was November 27th, 1978, and I was working the night shift. Hours earlier, George Moscone, the mayor of San Francisco, and Harvey Milk, an SF supervisor, were assassinated inside of City Hall. They were gunned down in cold blood by Dan White, a former city supervisor. The city reeled in shock and despair; riots broke out at the Civic Center in front of City Hall and a cloud of sadness and confusion hung over like a plague. George Moscone was a popular mayor and family man. Harvey Milk was a gay rights advocate who owned a camera store on Castro Street. Both men were in the prime of their lives. The news of this tragic event reverberated everywhere. It almost seemed as historic as I imagined the great earthquake of 1906 was. Most passengers I had that evening were talking about it, trying to process the chaos and disruption these murders had on San Franciscans…that is, most passengers until I met Travis.

Travis Bailey was a Black jazz musician. He was a trumpet player who was a regular in the Bay Area jazz scene for many years. He was probably in his late forties and had performed and recorded with some of the greats from coast to coast. Originally from Louisiana, he migrated to the Bay Area in the 1950s after serving in the U.S. Navy, stationed in Alameda. I picked Travis up around 2:00 a.m. in front of The Keystone Corner on Vallejo St.—one of the premier jazz venues in the city. The club had closed for the night, and he had just finished a gig there. He wanted to go to his home off Monterey Blvd. I drove down Broadway till I got on the Embarcadero freeway. It was a clear, brisk night and the stars twinkled like ornaments over the bay. There was little traffic and the city skyline looked like something out of a film noir, with lights peering out of buildings and dark shadows cast down eerily on the empty streets.

I had heard of Travis but never met him or saw him perform. When I mentioned the murders at City Hall, he didn't reply, just smoked a cigarette with the window open, wind whipping breezily across his face as he gazed out at the shimmering skyline. After a minute or so, he commented, "I've seen a lot of shit in my time, including riots and racial unrest. I grew up in the

South during the Jim Crow era and felt the pain and degradation of racial discrimination daily." He went on, "It's now 1978, ten years after Martin Luther King Jr's assassination, more than twenty years since the civil rights movement of the 1950s, yet Black mayoral representation in American cities are scant. Don't get me wrong, what happened yesterday at City Hall was a tragedy indeed. But in my mind, if it were a Black mayor who had been gunned down, it would have somehow been looked upon as just another incident at City Hall." He noted, "I wish I didn't feel that way, but I do; I just can't help it."

Manny the Hack

Manny Fein was a short, charismatic guy with a shit-eating grin that looked like he knew something about you that you didn't know about yourself. He was an owner/driver at Yellow Cab and probably the most popular hack in San Francisco. He had been a fixture on the streets for over twenty years. Most of the time, you could find Manny in front of the Sheraton Palace on New Montgomery St., holding court with other cabbies lined up in front of the hotel. It seemed everybody knew Manny and loved him. He was a friendly, fast-talking chain smoker originally from 110th and West End Avenue in Manhattan. He never lost his New York accent and always had a tale to tell about his life as a cab driver. I met Manny the first day I started driving a cab at the old Greyhound bus station on 7th St. He came over and introduced himself. He said, "I don't think I've ever seen you before." We shook hands and I said, "I'm Bill, today is my first shift driving."

"Nice to meet you, Bill." He stood near to me, looked up, and advised, "Whatever you do, Bill, don't get discouraged if you don't make much money the first day, first week, or even the first month. When you start driving a taxi in the city, you have to pay the dues till you get acquainted with the ins and outs of the business." I never forgot his advice, and from that moment on, he became one of my dearest friends.

Years later, Manny developed a cocaine habit that began to dominate his life. Everyone was aware of it and sometimes it was obvious by the white powdered circles encompassing his nostrils. He didn't just do the occasional snort now and then, it was daily, and lots of it, to the point that he started dealing it in order to keep up with his habit. There were three bars in the city he would deal out of. One of the bars was a joint I used to go to occasionally in North Beach. One night, his wife stormed into the bar, told him she had had enough of his coke habit, and said she was leaving him. They had battled about this for years and she was at her wits end. It was the first time I, or anyone else, ever saw Manny speechless. He tried to calm her down, but it seemed too little, too late…she was gone.

The marital split took its toll on Manny. Instead of stopping, he did even more cocaine and it began to affect his health—both physically and mentally. He was thin and gaunt. His demeanor went from perpetually upbeat to sad and beaten down. One night, he hit rock bottom and landed in the hospital with serious health issues resulting from years of abuse. He finally got help, quit the coke, quit the cigarettes, and after many years, got his life together. He remarried a woman he met in rehab and seemed happier and healthier than ever. He and his new wife traveled and made time to do all the things their addictions prevented them from doing. Life was good for Manny and you could see it on his face—he was back.

Then, early one morning, I got a phone call from a fellow cabbie who told me Manny had passed away in his sleep. I was stunned, shocked, and couldn't imagine not seeing him again. Not hearing his voice or laughter seemed unfathomable to me. The funeral was a week later. It seemed every cab driver in the city showed up to pay their respects, celebrate his indomitable spirit, and tell their favorite tale of a man who spread so much joy with his unique observations of life behind the wheel of a taxi. That was the beloved "Manny the Hack."

The News Anchors

F loyd Delburger and Jennifer Burns were the face of local news in the Greater Bay Area. They had been on the air together longer than any other news anchors and dominated the ratings among the other networks. Their public personas were plastered everywhere: billboards, the Sunday paper's magazine section, and television ads. They sponsored sports and charitable events all around the Bay Area and beyond. Their enormous presence was hard to avoid, and their popularity was unparalleled. They had an on-air demeanor of ease and humor that delighted viewers and made watching them an effortless task. Floyd Delburger had a medium build with thick brown hair that had a perpetual cowlick to it. He spoke with a deep voice of certainty and compassion and had a kind of golly-gee feel to his delivery. Jennifer Burns was probably in her forties and was easy on the eyes. She was tall and had jet black, shoulder length hair and bright blue eyes with long, complimenting eyelashes. She seemed to project an air of high morality and was not shy of alluding to her religious beliefs. Both were married with children that they often referred to affectionately in their newscasts. They were looked upon as dignified, clean-living San Franciscans, the kind of people you would want your children to grow up to emulate. They appeared to be models of respectability and decency, especially in a place as notoriously risqué as San Francisco…but that image was about to be shattered.

It was the last weekend before Christmas and holiday parties were plenty. I was driving down Powell Street near the St. Francis Hotel around 11 p.m. when I heard the consignors taxi whistle. I pulled over in front of the entrance and the doorman came over with a well-dressed couple and opened the back door for them. They got in and asked me to take them over the bridge, to a bar in Sausalito. I recognized the couple as Floyd and Jennifer from the local news station. They were friendly, giddy, touchy-feely, and veritably drunk. They had been at a holiday party for their station at the St Francis. As I drove through the steep and winding streets of the city, I could hear them talking and laughing expressively about the party. By the time I got on the Golden Gate Bridge, I could see in the rearview mirror that they had cozied up close to each other and the conversation had ceased. Then I heard them clamoring around in the backseat. She was cooing to Floyd, giving him the oohs and aahs— "Please, Floyd!" They were making out passionately.

    Her black hair was pulled back, her blouse unbuttoned. Floyd had his hand under her red lace bra and she was giggling with delight. Floyd was sweet talking to her with his pants down while Jen's red dress was up around her waist. They were going at it like drunken sailors, moaning and groaning, carrying on shamelessly, feeding their lust, adhering to their hormonal urges with reckless abandon, before I figured their guilt and remorseful regrets set in. I marveled how alcohol had stripped them of their public persona of decency and respectability. I felt like a fly on the wall hearing them get lost in their booze-fueled, inebriated fervor that undoubtedly will haunt them for years. I got to the bar on Bridgeway in Sausalito. The back door opened, and Jennifer was hooking her bra, buttoning her blouse, adjusting her dress, and combing her hair under the overhead light in the cab. Meanwhile, Floyd was zipping up his trousers, trying to tame his cowlick, straightening his tie and putting his loafers on. Still, they both looked drunk and disheveled, albeit postorgasmically. I couldn't wait to get back to the city and tell someone, anyone, anyone who'd listen. You'll never guess who I picked up.

San Francisco Woman

I've had a lot of strange and crazy people in my cab over the years, but Wanda was one of a kind. She was a middle-aged woman with a long face and oversized sunglasses that had masking tape on one temple to keep it in place. Her brunette hair was long, stringy, and dangled partly over her face. She wore a beat-up denim jacket with black jeans, red high top sneakers, and a white SF Giants cap. She wanted to go to a medical building on Sutter Street near Mt. Zion Hospital. She told me she had an appointment with her therapist and felt anxious about seeing him. "He doesn't seem to understand that the city of San Francisco is a woman, and I am that woman. In essence: I am San Francisco." I thought to myself, *Whoa, this ought to be interesting, tell me more…*She did.

I drove down Fulton Street and was all ears. She told me, "I've tried to explain to my therapist that I literally embody the city in many ways." I asked, "How so?"

"Well, take the way I look, for example. I can be as beautiful as a freshly painted Victorian on Steiner Street or as beautiful as the view of the bay from Telegraph Hill or any other vista in the city. I can also be as ugly as the sounds of garbage trucks in the early morning or trash lining the streets in the Tenderloin or near the Civic Center. I can also be as moody as the weather. I can be as sad and depressed as the morning fog hindering the sun or the whipping wind kicking up sand at the beach. I can cry like a rainstorm in January or laugh and sing like a warm sunny day in May. I can be as easy as lounging around in Washington Square, watching people throw a frisbee. I can be as destructive as an earthquake, as smart as the halls of all the universities and colleges in town, or as dumb as a bad idea out of City Hall."

She asked, "Am I making sense to you?" I thought for a moment and answered, "In many ways, you are." She seemed aware, but wounded, and as vulnerable as a nest of baby sparrows in a windstorm.

Wanda's mood began to change; she became sullen and introspective. She sat in the backseat, silently staring out the window, tears rolling slowly down her cheeks. She lit a cigarette and quietly mumbled to herself. I felt sorry for her. How difficult it must be to live with mood swings that scaled the heights and depths of human emotions. She clearly didn't have both oars in the water. As we got closer to her doctor's office, she said defiantly, "It can be both good and bad being the embodiment of San Francisco. Lots of people love it, lots of people don't—just like me. But I don't give a shit, this is who I am, and if my therapist doesn't want to accept that, he can go fuck himself. I'm not gonna change for him or anyone else."

When we got to her destination I pulled over and said, "Well, it was nice to meet you, Wanda. I hope everything goes all right with your doctor's visit." She didn't say anything and started getting out of the cab. I said, "Uh, Wanda, aren't you forgetting something?" She looked around in the backseat then said, "No."

I said, "You owe me $6.80." She glared at me and yelled, "I don't owe you anything!"

I replied, "There's $6.80 on the meter."

"So what!" she exclaimed. "I'm not paying you or anyone for driving on my streets. These streets are me, like everything else in this city. You haven't been listening, I am San Francisco!" Then she slammed the door and stormed away. I sat there and watched her march into the building. This woman was so crazy that she was convinced she was the essence of San Francisco, and for $6.80, I wasn't about to argue with her.

Another Day at the Office

Several people were lined up, waiting for a taxi in front of the train station. A tall man with dark glasses, sporting a black leather coat and carrying a large briefcase, made his way toward me. He peered inside for a long moment then got in the cab. He handed me a piece of paper with an address on it and asked, "Do you know where this is?" It was on Mt. Davidson, a residential neighborhood not far from Twin Peaks.

"Yes, it's on the other side of town, but I know exactly where it is."

"Good. Just let me know when you're about five minutes from the address."

TAXI VIGNETTES

"OK," I said, and drove out Market St. toward his destination. The man didn't say anything, just gazed out the window smoking a cigarette. We crossed Van Ness Avenue, Church St., and then Castro St. I continued up Market toward Twin Peaks and told him we were about five minutes away from his address. "OK," he replied, then directed: "I want you to listen closely to me. When we get on the street near the address, I want you to drive very slowly. I want you to look straight ahead, don't look back or in your rearview mirror—just straight ahead. Do you understand?" I nodded, yes.

He added, "When we get in front of the house, I want you to stop until I tell you to go. When I say go, drive me to the train station at Diamond and Chenery St.—do you know where that is?" I nodded yes again; it was just down the hill a few minutes away. I didn't ask any questions, I just complied with his directions. He spoke calmly, with a tone of authority and experience. I couldn't figure out who he was or what he did, but I was beginning to get the distinct feeling he'd done this before…whatever it was.

As we're approaching the street, I hear a strange noise from the backseat. It sounds like a clicking noise, like metal to metal or something of that order. I don't dare look back or in the rearview mirror. I'm beginning to feel anxious and have no inkling of what he's doing or what's about to happen. We get to the street, and I slow down to a crawl. It's a narrow, winding street with modest homes, probably constructed in the 1960s. There's little traffic, if any, and parked cars line the street on both sides. I look for the house address and find it. I stop and tell him, "This is it." He reiterates, "Just look straight ahead, driver, and do what I told you. Don't look back or at the house."

    I'm jittery, wondering what's gonna go down and if I'm gonna be harmed in any way. I look straight ahead, uneasy with this whole scenario. I hear him roll down the window. There's a short silent pause, then *BANG, BANG, BANG, BANG*. With each loud bang, I flinched, almost jumping out of my seat. Instinctively, I glance in the rearview mirror and at the house, then quickly turn my gaze straight ahead. I could see he shot up the front door to smithereens with a sawed-off shotgun—the thing I must have heard him assemble in the backseat.

    My heart is pounding, I'm speechless, not to mention scared as hell. He tells me, "Go!" I hit the gas and headed down the hill past the laundromat and grocery store on the corner, looking straight ahead, just like he wanted. I hear him disassemble the shotgun and stuff it in his briefcase. I turn left, roll through the stop sign, and get to the station at Diamond and Chenery. I pull up to the curb in front of the passenger zone. He throws a fat wad of cash over the seat, hops out of the cab with his briefcase in hand, and saunters off casually to the entrance, like it was just another day at the office.

www.ingramcontent.com/pod-product-compliance
Lightning Source LLC
LaVergne TN
LVHW051957060526
838201LV00059B/3699